Hurricane Juan
the story of a storm

Nimbus Publishing and The Herald, publisher of
The Chronicle-Herald, The Mail-Star and The Sunday Herald

Halifax, Nova Scotia
2003

Nimbus Publishing Limited
PO Box 9166
Halifax, NS   B3K 5M8
(902) 455-4286

Printed and bound in Canada

Design: Stephen Maher

National Library of Canada Cataloguing in Publication

Hurricane Juan : the story of a storm / the herald ; edited by Stephen Maher.
ISBN 1-55109-477-0

1. Hurricane Juan, 2003. 2. Hurricanes—Nova Scotia—Halifax Region. I. Maher, Stephen, 1965-

QC945.H87 2003   363.34'922'0971622
C2003-906268-6

Canada

The Canada Council | Le Conseil des Arts
for the Arts | du Canada

We acknowledge the financial support of the Government of Canada through the Book Publishing Industry Development Program (BPIDP) and the Canada Council for our publishing activities.

Contributors: Dan Arsenault, Patricia Brooks, Rick Conrad, Barry Dorey, Amy Pugsley Fraser, John Gillis, Eva Hoare, David Jackson, Davene Jeffrey, Randy Jones, Cathy von Kintzel, Tim Krochak, Christian Laforce, Lois Legge, Laurent Le Pierres, Mary Ellen MacIntyre, Bruce MacKinnon, Stephen Maher, Clare Mellor, Peter Parsons, Darren Pittman, Bill Power, Ted Pritchard, Steve Proctor, Kelly Shiers, Bill Spurr, Jennifer Stewart, Ralph Surette, Brian Underhill, Len Wagg, Beverley Ware, Eric Wynne
Editor: Stephen Maher
Copy editor: Liane Heller
Photo editor: Len Wagg
Design supervision: John Howitt
Thanks to: Dorothy Blythe, Susan Bradley, Steve Bruce, Heather Bryan, Fred Buckland, Tim Chisholm, Bev Dauphinee, Graham Dennis, Sarah Dennis, Frank DePalma, Chuck Douthwaite, Stu Ducklow, Mike Foran, Brian Freeman, Sheryl Grant, Mike Harvey, Bob Howse, Ken Jennex, Joel Jacobson, Darryl Kenty, Pat Lee, Kevin MacDonald, Sandra McIntyre, Terry O'Neil, Darren Pittman, Bill Richards, Christine Soucie, Dan Soucoup, Pam Sword, Vince Walsh, Deborah Wiles, Paul Williams
Special thanks: This book wouldn't have been possible without the extraordinary efforts of Lois Legge, Kelly Shiers and Liane Heller.
Cover photo: Fishermen reassemble their shattered wharf so they can get to their boat, Secondwind, in Herring Cove on Monday, Sept. 29. Photo by Tim Krochak.

Contents

Editor's Note/**IV**

The Storm/1

In the eye of hurricane Juan/**3**

The Damage/13

Après Juan, a deluge of sightseers/**32**
A walk through a strange, silent city/**36**
For fishermen, absolute devastation/**39**
Heartbreaking damage on the farm/**42**
In parks and woods, arboreal carnage/**45**

Tragedy/49

Falling trees take two lives/**50**
'Mary is gone to make flowers'/**52**

Coping/53

Born in the teeth of a gale/**54**
A reminder to live life to the fullest/**55**
'This brought out the best in us'/**57**
Hungry for power, with no excuse/**58**
Heck, that wasn't so bad/**59**
A struggle to feed the hungry/**60**
Milk (and bacon) of human kindness/**61**
When the going gets tough ... /**62**
After Juan, generosity of spirit/**64**
'My mom said we'd better pray'/**66**

Recovery/67

A power struggle of epic proportions/**69**
It left a really, really, really big mess/**73**
Waiting for the next crop of trees/**74**

Editor's note

A few days after hurricane Juan, a handful of e-mail printouts appeared on the bulletin board in The Herald newsroom.

They were notes from people writing to thank us — for our coverage of the storm and for getting the paper to them on the morning after hurricane Juan, even though the streets were clogged with trees and downed power lines. That the paper was there, when everything had been torn to pieces, was a comfort to readers. And the information it contained was vital, since most people still didn't have electricity.

We didn't get the paper to all our subscribers, but our circulation department did everything in its power to get it to everyone we could reach.

The reporters, editors and photographers who stayed on through the storm did all they could, working with desperate efficiency on generator-powered computers, even as windows blew out in The Herald building on Argyle Street. One editor,

not realizing how bad it really was outside, tried to drive home to Dartmouth during the storm. She ended up stranded by deadfalls on a Halifax side street, where some kind people — Newfoundlanders, as it happens — invited her in. She spent the night on their couch.

The story of reporter Amy Pugsley Fraser's harrowing journey home to her family appears elsewhere in this book.

In the days that followed, everyone at The Herald rallied to cover the storm, and to get the paper out every day. Reporters, editors, photographers, technicians, secretaries, cleaners, carpenters, compositors, managers and delivery people all left their ravaged neighbourhoods and drove down dangerous streets to the office because we had to put out the paper. Their families had to deal with the mess at home. Almost everybody was living without electricity. Many were living without phone service or water.

They complained about all that, but I didn't hear anyone complain about the work. Here's why: We are lucky to do it. It is important, satisfying, creative work. We provide a service to the people of Nova Scotia, and we are proud of it.

Pride is a strong emotion. It can get you out of bed before dawn, get you to pick up your flashlight and walk to the bathroom through the darkness. It can make you have an icy shower in the darkness so that you can get dressed, leave your family sleeping and make your way to the office.

I think you see that pride in this book, which was produced very quickly under difficult circumstances by the talented, tired, hard-working, stressed-out people of The Herald.

It is our record of hurricane Juan.

All of The Herald's profits will go to the Canadian Red Cross Disaster Services Program.

—**Stephen Maher**

The Storm

Two swimmers wade into the surf churned up by the leading edge of hurricane Juan at Lawrencetown Beach on Sunday, hours before the storm hit.

In the eye of hurricane Juan

It was born a number, not a name.

At noon on Thursday, Sept. 25, the mass of clouds 470 kilometres southeast of Bermuda was dubbed Tropical Depression No. 15 by the National Hurricane Center in Miami.

By 6 p.m., No. 15 was 325 kilometres southeast of the island, gathering force. It was now a tropical storm. And the centre gave it a name.

Juan.

By suppertime Friday, it had become an intense, rotating oceanic weather system with maximum sustained winds exceeding 119 kilometres per hour.

A hurricane.

Juan was now 255 kilometres east of Bermuda, and forecasters tracked it with mounting concentration as it closed in on Nova Scotia's coast.

By 9 p.m. Friday, the Canadian Hurricane Centre in Dartmouth was predicting Juan could make landfall in Nova Scotia on Sunday and was warning of heavy rain and strong winds for the province.

On Saturday at 3 a.m., the centre was more specific — 50 to 80 millimetres of rain and gusts of 100 to 120 km/h. By 9 a.m., the report warned that Juan would cause local flooding and topple trees, knocking out power.

The bulletin at 3 a.m. Sunday added some grim new information: THE NEAR COINCIDENCE OF THE STORM SURGE WITH THIS HIGH TIDE WILL LIKELY LEAD TO SOME COASTAL FLOODING, INCLUDING POSSIBLY THE DOWNTOWN WATERFRONT OF HALIFAX.

On Monday, Sept. 29, 2003, at 12:10 a.m., Juan crashed ashore between the fishing communities of Prospect and Shad Bay, Halifax County.

It was the worst hurricane to hit the province since the Second Great August Gale of 1893 killed 25 people.

Juan barrelled toward Halifax, its winds pack-

The storm begins to form on the afternoon of Sept. 25.

NOAA / PHOTO OPPOSITE: TIM KROCHAK

ing such a wallop forecasters considered upping it from a Category 1, the mildest of five levels (up to 150 km/h), to a Category 2 (up to 175 km/h).

Death rode in the fury of Juan's winds, which topped 150 km/h, gusting to 176 km/h at McNabs Island in Halifax Harbour. Generations-old trees strained to stay rooted but failed, with tragic consequences. Families would be left to mourn two men killed inside vehicles that were crushed by falling trees.

More than two-thirds of all the trees in historic Point Pleasant Park, a forest oasis in the provincial capital, were pulverized. The beloved Public Gardens was in ruins. Sidewalks crumbled as massive roots heaved out of the ground. Houses faltered under the weight of trees. Yards were stripped bare.

Storm surges — caused when hurricanes suck up water, raising the ocean's level — were as high as 1.5 metres. Fishermen lost their gear, their boats, their sheds, their wharfs, only weeks before the lucrative fall lobster season was to open. Farmers and foresters faced catastrophe.

Hundreds abandoned their homes as waterfront properties flooded. Boat owners were helpless as the storm ripped vessels from their docks.

Across the region, boats sank. Others were found far away. At the Northwest Arm in Halifax, three boats dragged their moorings and crashed ashore on Horseshoe Island.

In all, 85 millimetres of rain pelted the region. Canadian National lost 1,300 metres of track, and 10 cars derailed in the deluge. In Halifax Regional Municipality, a state of emergency was declared.

At his Pictou County home, Nova Scotia Premier John Hamm knew the situation in Halifax was grim long before the linden tree he planted 30 years ago crashed over his driveway. He heard the news from Ernie Fage, the minister responsible for the province's Emergency Measures Act, who called after midnight.

"He was telling me that ... our worst fears were being realized."

Ron Duggan looked hurricane Juan in the eye. And lived to tell the tale.

The howling winds slapped his skin and he tasted the salty sea spray as the tempest touched down in Prospect, a pretty fishing village of wooden houses built around a granite cove at the end of a peninsula stretching into the Atlantic. That the cove is sheltered by islands at the mouth of Prospect Bay did nothing to curb Juan.

The ocean was literally chasing the 70-year-old fisherman; the waves lapped at his heels as he ran from the fiercest storm in memory.

It was about 12:30 a.m., Sept. 29. Hurricane Juan had slammed down between Shad Bay and Prospect just 20 minutes earlier. Now it tore through Prospect, its 140 km/h wind tossing wharfs and boats into the air like toys as it raged toward Halifax. Everything seemed to be on fast-forward. The ocean rushed to shore; the trees swung to and fro in a demented dance that would leave them limp, broken or flat on the ground.

But Ron and his younger brother, Joe — who'd come in from his Mount Uniacke home to check on his gear — had to keep their livelihoods afloat. Their fishing boats, lobster traps and wharfs, awaiting the November fishing season, could all be lost.

Minutes before Ron ventured out into the violent winds, his oceanfront house rattling and shaking as if possessed, his brother had stormed through the door. Joe was soaked, sheet-white and frantic after battling to protect his boat and lobster gear. His truck had got stuck in the driveway at the edge of the wharf. Logs and planks from now-shattered buildings and wharfs blocked his way. The ocean, whipped into a frenzy, closed in around him.

"I had to hang onto the wheel," Joe remembers. "The truck felt like it was going to blow over, it was blowing so hard. So I got out, and when I did I realized the water was up to my waist. So I went up through the field and left the truck there.

"I had to crawl up through because I couldn't see. There was no power, no lights. (I was) crawling up through the trees, trying to feel my way through."

Joe, 57, made his way back about 180 metres to his brother's house.

Now it was Ron's turn to face a storm ferocious enough to leave even veteran fishermen in awe.

"It was crazy," says Ron, a sturdily built former Halifax police officer who's been a lobster fisherman since his retirement 15 years ago.

"We shouldn't have been there, I suppose. But you don't know that, you know? You're thinking, hey, there's something I've worked for all my life

The storm takes shape on the afternoon of Sept. 26.

... and I'm going to lose it."

He and Joe had been fishing since they were boys. Their father, a fisherman and boat builder, had taught them how, passing on a trade that had been in the family for generations.

So Ron went back out with his brother, the wind flapping at his rain jacket, his tuque blowing off so often he jammed it in his pocket, and tried to stand firm in his rubber boots.

"It was almost impossible to stand against it with the gust that hit," Ron says. "It's one of the strongest winds I've experienced."

They struggled to nail a door shut on a shed about 10 metres from his house. The vicious wind had already shattered its windows.

"My brother said to me, 'Just taste the salt' — the rain hitting your face, and it was pure salt," Ron recalls.

Using flashlights, they rushed back to the water's edge to retrieve the truck.

It was close to 1 a.m., and "there was nothing left, all the wharfs and all the fishing sheds," says Ron. "Everything was gone."

He recalls the sucking sounds of the waves

rushing in and out as the two of them quickly removed the wharf pilings, fallen spruce shingles, planks and logs blocking their path.

"I knew that the tide runs in, then it sucks back out really heavy and if you can get in, in that interim, we could get his truck out of there," Ron says.

"So this is what we worked on and we started to back it" — Ron directing his brother with a flashlight from outside.

The elder brother chuckles in anticipation of his next memory — a laugh halfway between amusement and awe.

"Suddenly," he says, "I heard the water rushing in again, so I started to run and it was on my heels and it was getting deeper, and I was able to get to a house that had a veranda on it and I ran up there and it was still licking at my heels.

"It came in and sucked back out again and I ran down and I waved to him, and he was able to bring the truck back out."

They returned to Ron's house for a breather and change of boots. Then, hoping to find some remnant of their battered gear, the brothers stepped out into the raging night once again.

"We got back over to the main paved road and we went down looking for our boats, and there they were, lo and behold, sitting high and dry," Ron recalls.

But their lobster traps weren't spared. Most of the ones that weren't washed out to sea turned up the next day, battered and twisted beyond repair. The crippling wind mangled their wharfs too. Sitting in his truck that night, Joe thinks he might have seen the roof of Ron's wharf sailing by in the sky — then, a domino effect, as others along the shore flew off.

By 2:30 a.m., drowning their sorrows seemed the only thing left to do.

"I think it took us 30 minutes to drink three bottles of wine," Ron recalls with a laugh.

"Years ago when (storms) used to come, they always left something, whether it needed to be repaired or not. But this time it cleaned everything."

Almost.

A windsurfer gets dumped from his board while taking advantage of the wind and waves off Grand Desert on Sunday evening as Juan neared Nova Scotia.

TIM KROCHAK

Joe was relieved to see something left in the eye of the storm. "There was still a star up there anyway — that didn't blow away."

Hurricane Juan wrapped its winds around Chris Fogarty.

But he didn't have to look up.

He was travelling through the eye of the storm in a Convair 580, a twin-engine turboprop, its belly full of scientific instruments, computers and electronic equipment anchored to metal shelving.

It all trembled as the plane shook in the sky like a car on a dirt road.

Chris saw a sight few could imagine — an almost cartoon-like chasm in the air.

"When we get to the eye of the storm, we can see the rain stop just like a wall — a vertical wall of rain," says the Canadian Hurricane Centre meteorologist, who was in the air for four hours.

Chris was getting wind, temperature and humidity readings from some of the plane's drop-sondes, instrument packages that transmit measurements to the aircraft as they fall through the storm, guided by little parachutes.

"We dropped one just on the north side of the eye and another one on the south side," says Chris, who was part of an eight-member crew, including scientists from the National Research Council.

"We're seeing extremely high winds the further this thing goes down. The winds are increasing, increasing to about ... 180, 190 kilometres an hour. Those winds are almost near the ground, as you can tell by all the damage."

But those winds didn't touch the ground. The measurements came from the base of the clouds, where speeds are higher than the ground-level gales used to define hurricane categories.

"Even the treetops themselves would have been experiencing ... at least five, 10 per cent higher wind gusts — enough to push them down."

Still, Chris knew things were bad below.

Wind speeds were intense as the research council's airplane chased the storm right off the coast of Prospect. So Chris wasn't surprised by what he heard when he called his colleagues at the hurricane centre sometime between 12:30 and 1 a.m. on Monday, Sept. 29. "They said, 'We're down in the lobby now.' "

The staffers had just descended the steps of their office tower in the dark.

Chris, a bespectacled, sandy-haired man of 29, had been at the centre all day Sunday, until the takeoff from Halifax International Airport at about 10 p.m.

He'd worried that the top-floor windows of the waterfront building might blow in. The centre is housed in Queen Square, a brick and glass structure in downtown Dartmouth, exposed to the harbour. "We had big strips of tape over the windows" to protect against the expected onslaught.

But by 12:20 a.m. Juan came knocking hard enough to cut off the building's power; an emergency generator for the centre's 19th-floor office kicked in. And the tower was trembling.

"We have almost floor-to-ceiling windows; it was noisy," remembers centre meteorologist and office manager Ken Kirkwood. "You could hear the wind howling. You could hear things banging. You could feel a slight sway."

None of the hurricane watchers or Maritime Weather Centre employees, just cubicles away, mentioned it then. They were caught up in getting information to the public and taking the near-constant calls from the media.

But at about 12:30 a.m., a tile popped from the office's suspended ceiling — the result, Ken thinks, of a wind-funnelling effect around the building.

The centre put its contingency plan into action.

Environment Canada weather centres in Gander, Nfld., and Fredericton, N.B. (where a hurricane specialist had been dispatched the day before), would temporarily take over.

Ken and his colleagues made their way down darkened stairs to the 16th floor, which, unlike their office, didn't have emergency power. The windows whistled and shook there, too.

"We thought ... maybe the best place to go is to the stairwell," he recalls. "So we went to the stairwell, and that's where people noticed the building swaying, and so we decided to go down to the ground floor."

Employees returned to the top floor by 1:15 a.m., when winds in the Halifax area started dying down. By that time, Chris and the crew were thinking about a place to land. Winds were still too high at the Halifax airport and picking up in Sydney. The pilot decided to land in Stephenville, Nfld.

That's when Chris called his parents back in New Glasgow, where as a boy he'd marvelled at the area's windstorms.

He knew they'd be worried about the son they think is just a little bit crazy, the son so fascinated by the storms he once ran through hurricane Hortense in downtown Halifax, just to see how it would feel.

"They probably would have killed me if I didn't call," he says. "The storm was just hitting New Glasgow full force at that point, and they were describing (it), saying, 'Holy cow, the willow tree just broke in half.' I could hear the wind on the phone."

Sometime around 1 a.m., Chris Tanner was wrenched from sleep by a noise so unfamiliar she still struggles to describe it.

"Have you seen the movie Titanic, when the ship started coming apart? That creaking noise, that's the first thing I thought of," the 27-year-old would later recall.

She realized the power was out as she made her way to the bathroom, trying not to bump into the walls of the Dartmouth apartment she shared with her partner, Rebekah Looby, 21, who was still asleep. She looked outside. The downpour was "like someone throwing buckets of water at the window."

Chris considered going into the dining room where she could open the door to the outside hallway to see if the emergency lights were still working. But she decided against it.

Afraid, the slender woman with short brown

Hurricane Juan closes in on Nova Scotia in a satellite photo taken at 2:45 p.m. on Sunday, Sept. 28. By then, forecasters were predicting flooding in downtown Halifax.

hair woke up her partner. "Can't you hear it? Isn't it scary?" Chris cried.

"She said, 'We'll be all right. We have guardian angels looking after us.'

"And I swear, not even a minute later, it just went boom, right out of nowhere. The roof just fell right on us."

Just a few hours earlier, the two women had been playing crazy eights. Now they feared for their lives.

Rebekah and Chris, a Mount Saint Vincent University student, had lived in their third-floor apartment on Windmill Road in Dartmouth for about six months. They'd been attracted by its size — big enough for all their stuff, plus two cats and a rabbit — and the balcony view of the busy harbour. But on Sunday night, with the curtain closed, they weren't paying attention to the view at all. Neither of them noticed the rain begin or the winds ominously gathering strength.

By about 10:30 p.m., they were sound asleep. But for Chris's need for reassurance, Rebekah might still have been sleeping when their bedroom ceiling crashed and the entire roof caved in over their dining room, opening it to the nightmarish sky.

The storm had whacked the side of the higher building attached to theirs, exposing rafters and ventilation systems, sending bricks and wood crashing down through the roof of their home.

The noise sliced through the night. They felt debris bounce off their shoulders and backs. Bits of insulation, concrete, drywall and wood crashed down, blocking the only door.

Pipes in the ceiling tore open, releasing a torrent of water that washed over their bare feet and flooded the room ankle-deep, then rose to mid-shin.

They screamed. Chris considered jumping out the window, thinking a broken leg might not be as bad as staying put. But the window provided another, less painful, opportunity. Through it, they could see people across the courtyard. They yelled for help.

"In about 10 minutes, two young fellows came out, and they waved up, and I yelled out the apart-

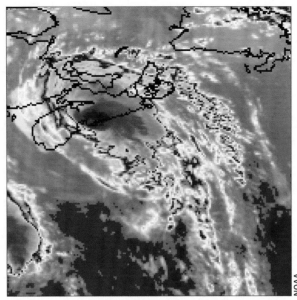

Hurricane Juan covers much of Nova Scotia in this infrared photo from the small hours of Sept. 29.

ment number: 'Three-four-three!' I was screaming, the wind was so loud and I don't know how he heard us. But he yelled back, 'Three-four-three!' — slow, like I did. And then he said, 'OK. We're going to get help.' "

As they waited, Rebekah grabbed the dowelling from the window and battered a hole in the bedroom wall, breaking through into the spare bedroom.

There, Chris, dressed only in jogging pants and a sweater, and Rebekah, in her nightdress and jeans, hoped rescuers would find them. Twenty more minutes would pass before they heard a voice, "Is anybody there?" A police officer had arrived through the rubble.

Without shoes, there was no way the women — now with one of their cats, the other missing in the chaos — could follow him back over the mess.

The officer began to kick at a wall, smashing a way out of the room. Then, seizing a pickle barrel from the apartment, he and another officer beat through one more wall into the next apart-

ment. From there, they could get to a stairwell that would lead them to safety.

By 2 a.m., worn and weary, the two were on a Metro Transit bus bound for a comfort station that had been set up in the nearby Dartmouth Sportsplex.

But they didn't stay. Rebekah wasn't feeling well. By 4 a.m., she was taken by ambulance to hospital, where she was treated for nausea and shock.

Later that morning, Chris would return to the ruined apartment to look for their driver's licences, bank cards and identification. She found none. She did, however, find their second cat, safe in the debris. The pet rabbit would later be found alive and well in its crushed cage.

Fear is a lasting memory.

There's fear of the dark. Fear of what your eyes strain to see but can't quite make out. Fear of what you can't hear, overwhelmed by the sound of the wind's assault on your ears.

And there's the fear of flying rocks and shattered glass that swirls around you. Fear of fallen trees that block your way and the fear of electrocution from snapped wires that dangle and twist in the wind.

Then there's the fear that comes as you understand that, yes, you've made it home safely, but the trek wasn't worth the risk.

"I don't think I've ever been more terrified in my life," Herald reporter Amy Pugsley Fraser, 35, says of her dash to her west-end Halifax home at the height of hurricane Juan. "It was like a nightmare — one of those ones where you're running, but you're standing still."

Almost 12 hours earlier, Amy made the four-minute drive from home to begin her Sunday afternoon shift at The Herald's downtown office, a four-storey concrete building that takes up a block of downtown Halifax. She would normally finish work by 9 p.m., but with hurricane Juan approaching, she thought she might be a bit later than usual.

There would be nothing usual about this shift.

Crowds of exuberant young people headed for the Halifax waterfront to test the strong winds late Sunday night as hurricane Juan approached the city.

TED PRITCHARD

At times, she knelt beside filing cabinets as wind hurled gravel from nearby flat-roofed buildings against the office windows with machine-gun fury, breaking a pane on the floor above and sending composing-room staff fleeing for safety.

But still, Amy was probably in one of the safest places in Halifax that night. A generator was powering the lights, computers and fax machines. Only when she left the office did she realize how sheltered she and her co-workers had been from Juan's wrath.

All night long, she and fellow reporter Davene Jeffrey had monitored what was happening around them.

They were in contact with the Canadian Hurricane Centre on the other side of Halifax Harbour. They were also speaking with Halifax Mayor Peter Kelly and other officials to get updates from the emergency operations centre. With a scanner, they could listen to police, fire and other municipal staff radioing each other from around the region.

The extent of Juan's force was apparent hours before it made landfall: Halifax was in a state of emergency. Waterfront buildings and homes were evacuated. There were downed power lines and waves crashing over seawalls, wiping out wharfs and boardwalks along the coast.

Then, at about 1 a.m. Monday, news came that a Dartmouth apartment building had collapsed.

"When one of the calls on the radio was to please be careful with the fire trucks because the apparatus could get stuck in the wires, that's when we knew things were very dangerous," recalls Amy, a slim reporter with shoulder-length blond hair.

She would soon experience just how dangerous things really were.

Amy had wanted to leave since 12:30 a.m. She'd been speaking on the phone with her husband, Hugh, who was at home with their two young sons.

She knew the power was out and a tree had crashed into the back porch. Without lights, it was impossible for Hugh to see what damage it had caused.

A computer graphic from the hurricane centre that showed Juan still directly overhead persuaded her to wait a bit longer. But in a half-hour, Amy was still anxious to get home to her family and decided against staying at a nearby hotel with Davene and other colleagues.

She set out at about 1:10 a.m. Normally, even on a Sunday night, there would be people out and about, meandering from bars to restaurants and back again.

Not on Sept. 29.

"The most startling thing was opening the door to Argyle Street, and thinking, 'The power's off everywhere. The generator in our building was the only source of power.'

"It was pitch-dark, but there was an eerie glow in the sky, broken glass all over the sidewalk and a bizarre sound — I only figured out a week later — of the wind whipping the metal rings on (The Herald's) flagpoles, like the sound of a buoy out in the middle of the harbour."

The wind was fierce, and she braced herself against the onslaught. But the uphill walk to her van was only the start of her struggle.

As she drove, the van's headlights shone through the mist, barely illuminating the destruction. She passed Royal Artillery Park, negotiating a slalom course of giant trees that crossed Sackville Street.

"The Public Gardens was worse. It's seeing things where they shouldn't be and knowing that these were beautiful trees, and they were lying on the road. They were huge, so there was just enough room to get past the tips of the branches, driving very close to the sidewalk."

Amy's route was taking her to Summer Street. But as she neared that road, she saw a man with a flashlight on the corner by Camp Hill Cemetery, walking toward her, motioning her to detour.

She could see trees lying everywhere and a tangled web of wires that brushed the sidewalks. What she couldn't tell, but would later learn, is that she had just come across tragedy.

Minutes before, paramedic John Rossiter had died at the intersection of Summer and Veterans

Memorial Lane, crushed by the weight of a falling tree as he sat in the rear of an ambulance.

Unaware of the horror, she attempted another route, only to learn a tree was blocking that path as well. "I thought maybe I would have more luck on foot; I could get through places a car can't."

Leaving the van at the CBC Television building, she declined the offer of journalists still covering the storm to wait out the hurricane with them. Instead, she decided to make a run for home, just seven blocks away.

"It must have been raining quite hard, but the primary thing I remember was the wind. It was deafening ... inescapable, constantly coming at you .... I was running uphill, taking shallow breaths, almost hyperventilating."

With just a block to go, there was more fear.

"I knew there were at least three or four trees on the street between me and my door, and I couldn't tell where they were."

She continued on. A half-hour after she left the office, she shut her home's front door behind her. She breathed a sigh of relief. Her family was safe. She was safe. And their house was fine. They'd collect the van later.

Halifax Mayor Peter Kelly wore two hats the night of the hurricane.

As husband to Nancy and father to 13-year-old Craig and nine-year-old Blake, he had taken precautions around their Bedford home the afternoon before.

He secured the house, tied down the barbecue and moved the lawn furniture before leaving the family to ride out the storm without him. Of course he was concerned about them. But he also had responsibilities to a community about to be hammered by hurricane Juan.

Halifax Regional Municipality was at the eye of the storm, and its mayor was at the centre of government response: the emergency operations centre on the Dartmouth side of the harbour.

Peter didn't spend the night with his family. He holed up at the emergency centre with fire, police and municipal staff, and representatives of the

There was a carnival atmosphere near Bishop's Landing on the Halifax waterfront at about 10:30 p.m. on Sunday. That changed when Juan arrived in full force.

TED PRITCHARD

federal, provincial and municipal emergency measures organizations awaiting updates from all over the region.

They monitored the evacuation of people from coastal and flood-prone areas. They heard reports of roofs being blown from buildings, of wide-spread power outages. They co-ordinated their responses. They set up places where evacuees could find comfort and safety.

Destruction was mounting. But death was the worst news — the paramedic's death, and that of a man in Hants County, also killed when a tree struck his vehicle.

"We were understanding the actual impact this was having on individuals, on their families and their co-workers," the mayor recalls.

He called home several times but got no answer. He comforted himself by assuming everything was OK. It would be 4 a.m. before his calls were answered and he knew for certain that his family was fine.

Jim Lorraine saw disaster from the seat of a farm tractor.

It was 4 a.m., and the winds and rain that blasted his family's farm in Upper Onslow, Colchester County, had finally died down enough for him to venture outside.

Anxiously, he looked over the two-storey home, where his wife, Tricia, and their three children — five-year-old Nicholas, two-year-old Eryn and baby Jill, not yet three months — were safely inside. It looked intact. And in the yard, he noticed only that the kids' playset had been knocked over.

The fit 34-year-old with short dark hair started up the tractor, thinking he'd head to the family's store to see how that had fared.

He soon realized there was no way he could steer around the downed trees and telephone lines that filled the road. He detoured through the fields that have been part of his family's farm for 200 years.

As he made his way, the tractor's lights picked up the farm's greenhouse in the distance.

It too was intact.

But it was in the wrong place.

"The wind had picked up the whole structure and carried it a few hundred feet, took out a few telephone poles along the way, a few trees, and it landed on the road."

It was only the beginning of the bad news.

When you farm for a living, weather can be your best friend. Or your worst enemy.

Regardless, it's a constant companion, ignored at your peril.

Because of that, the Lorraines kept close watch on hurricane Juan, following its track on the Internet, as it bore down on this province.

They had reason to worry. They knew their 500,000-stalk corn maze — an attraction that brought paying visitors to the farm — could be levelled in an instant by an angry wind.

Any other year, that would be bad news. This year, it could be disastrous.

It had been a particularly hard season for the Lorraines, who were named Atlantic Canada's Outstanding Young Farmers of 2002.

In March, floods wiped out 90 per cent of their strawberry plants.

Then, less than two months before the hurricane, an early frost killed off the sweet corn at the peak of the season.

Yet early Sunday evening, even as he made the rounds of the farm to close the doors of the barns, Jim was his naturally optimistic self. It was 7 p.m., the time forecasters had once predicted Juan would hit the Halifax area, and here, about 100 kilometres from the capital, there was only a breeze blowing.

Maybe the hurricane would pass by, he thought. Or, at least, its winds would lose force. Maybe it wouldn't be so bad.

By 8 p.m., the kids were sleeping upstairs in their bedrooms. Always prepared, the couple had flashlights at the ready. The wind had picked up a bit and it had started to rain. But there didn't seem any reason to keep watch. By 11 p.m., they too were asleep.

Just after 1 a.m., everything changed.

"We heard it. It woke us up. We could hear the rain pounding, the wind beating on the house. We went to the windows and you could see the trees blowing like you've never seen them blow before," Jim recalls.

By 1:30 a.m., the family was gathered together in a little room off the main part of their home. They thought they'd be safer there, buffered from any falling trees.

They tried to keep the older children amused by letting them play with flashlights — anything to get their minds off the storm.

Circling winds howled and whistled, hurling even the back-door thermometer around the house to the opposite corner where, in amazement, Jim would find it days later.

He went to a window in another room, shining his flashlight through the glass to try to see the barnyard.

"I realized when I had the flashlight to the window, the window was hitting the flashlight, and I was about an inch away. The window was bowing in and out that much."

There was nothing to do but wait a couple more hours until he could safely go outside and take a look at the damage.

There would be a lot of damage.

The corn maze was beaten to ruin. The cow corn crop was flattened. The observation beehive and strawberry booth were smashed. A barn was missing its roof. A cattle trailer was thrown onto its side. Part of an equipment shed was heaved out of the ground.

And just when they thought it couldn't get any worse, they learned that a local restaurant, their best customer for ground beef, had burned.

In those first hours of tallying the destruction, Jim couldn't help but wonder whether the family farm would survive.

But as the sun came up on Monday, Sept. 29, 2003, Jim was certain of one thing: "I refuse to lose, to be honest. And that's our whole philosophy .... There are a lot of people in the same boat, and we're going to have to somehow come out of it."

—Lois Legge and Kelly Shiers

The Damage

A man grins as he wades through knee-deep flood water on Robie Street near the Halifax Common on Monday morning.

A woman keeps her sweater over her head in the early morning rain on Cogswell Street in Halifax on Monday. The street was nearly impassable to vehicles.

A man walks across a jumble of yachts at the Dartmouth Yacht Club on Monday morning.

Cars roll past a row of fallen power poles and trees on Boland Street in Dartmouth early Monday.

Two girls make their way over a sidewalk pulled up by a fallen tree on Beech Street in Halifax.

Juan tore the Hector away from its dock in Pictou and drove it onto the rocks nearby. The ship is a replica of the vessel that brought the town's first settlers in 1773.

PETER PARSONS / PHOTO OPPOSITE: DARREN PITTMAN

Cars travelling on Highway 2 in Grand Lake veer to avoid a black spruce blown over by Juan.

June Hartling and her granddaughter, Chantelle Francis, look at the roof of a nearby apartment building outside their trailer on Bridget Avenue in Spryfield.

DARREN PITTMAN

The masts of Larinda stick out of the water early Monday. Larry Mahan of Cape Cod spent 30 years building the boat. It was raised from the harbour floor on Oct. 17.

A man on a motorized scooter and a cyclist travel on Barrington Street at about 7:30 Monday morning. The street was littered with debris from a construction project.

PETER PARSONS

The tide surge from Juan lifted long sections of the boardwalk on the Halifax waterfront and pushed them inland or swept them away.

Chunks of torn-up wharfs came to rest beside the Wave sculpture on the Halifax waterfront.

DARREN PITTMAN

Workers run straps around an 18-wheeler that flipped on Highway 102 near Enfield during the hurricane.

LEN WAGG

Broken windows gape in the Joseph Howe Building in downtown Halifax early Monday. Glass littered the sidewalks and streets nearby.

Gerri Elliott clears broken branches from Willow Street early Monday. Many of Halifax's streets were buried under mounds of broken branches.

Pedestrians had to walk on Barrington Street on Monday to avoid roof debris blown onto the street by hurricane Juan and moved to the sidewalk by cleanup workers.

Workers use a crane to try to right a tanker at a rail yard in Dartmouth on Monday. Juan damaged more than a kilometre of track and caused a 10-car derailment.

PETER PARSONS

Juan's surging tide pushed these sailboats — dragging their concrete moorings — from the Waegwoltic Club to Horseshoe Island in the Northwest Arm.

Après Juan, a deluge of sightseers

A family strolls in the front yard of a Bedford home dwarfed by a huge uprooted oak.

Halifax was made up of two main groups the morning after Juan: those who walked the streets to see what they could see and those who stayed at home to see what they could saw. In the heavily treed west and south ends, camera-toting gawkers exchanged tips on where to take in the most spectacular damage.

"Have you seen Vernon Street?" asked one. "You've got to go over there."

In the Westmount subdivision, John Bishop stood and gazed at the plastic bag that used to be his daughter Danielle's bedroom window.

"That pointed part up there came right down and jammed into that window not 10 minutes after we moved our daughter, who has a bed right under it," Mr. Bishop said.

"It was just like a spear went through it, and then the glass exploded. Those are all pressure-treated windows with argon gas in the middle of the two panes, so it just shattered. The whole room was full of glass."

The branch came through the window at about 2:30 a.m., and by then Mr. Bishop was expecting the combination of wind and big, mature trees to be a problem.

"To watch the wind blow these trees, it looked like the Friendly Giant had taken his hands and rubbed them right up to the tops of the trees, because when the wind came it just pushed everything up and then out," he said.

On Cedar Street, one man was guiding people to his neighbour's house, where a massive linden tree had uprooted, gouging a swath of earth, roots, pavement and concrete curb more than five metres across.

Flat stones in neat rows underneath had a woman speculating she had discovered an old makeshift sidewalk.

Later in the day, neighbours gathered in front of a darkened Cedar Street home for a barbecue.

The power was still out, but propane powered a hot meal for the families.

Others trekked downtown, where a well-lit city centre offered the promise of hot coffee and hot meals. So many food-seeking pilgrims arrived that at least one restaurant ran out of food by 10:30 p.m.

Clarence and Carole David of D'Escousse, in Halifax for several days visiting his daughter and new grandchild, finally got some hot food and coffee late in the day.

"The day started off with peanut butter sandwiches," Mr. David said. "And cold coffee," chimed in his wife.

The couple had been staying at a Quinpool Road flat, but Juan knocked out a window and sent a tree crashing across power lines.

"The City of Trees got hit last night, I'd say," a man walking down the street said, surveying an intersection where drivers turning off Jubilee Road in any direction were turned back by giant trees lying across the streets.

A huge toppled maple tree covered most of Barbara McLennan's Connaught Avenue home, but she said the damage seemed minimal.

"I don't think there's any damage to the house — it's the eavestrough, and one of the windows got broken."

She said the power went out around midnight and the winds were "just shaking the whole house."

"I thought the roof had come off."

On Willow Street, Seth Smith and roommate Paul Hammond had a huge cedar tree fall and poke through an upstairs window.

"We were on the other side of the house," Mr. Smith said. "There was just like this huge crash."

There was also a crash outside a home on Shirley Street, where a big window on the third

Liverpool Street residents look in amazement Monday at an enormous tree knocked down by Juan.

PETER PARSONS

A massive tree and a power pole both hit this Chevy Cavalier on Pepperell Street in Halifax.

floor was torn loose and shattered on the sidewalk. But the owner was foggy on the details.

"I don't even know what time that happened because I slept through the whole friggin' thing," he said. "I'm (ticked) right off. Missed the storm of the century."

On Oxford Street, five teenage girls smiled and posed for a photo in front of a home where the lawn was a tangle of power poles, downed lines and splintered trees.

Just down the street, the glass wall of a bus stop had been blown to smithereens, the Professional Centre at the corner of Robie and Spring Garden had windows missing from offices on the 10th, 11th and 12th floors, and at the Public Gardens, a crowd stood at the gates and gazed at the wreckage inside.

A tour of the Northwest Arm showed that some boat owners found out the term "land yacht" doesn't always refer to old Cadillacs.

The marina at the Royal Nova Scotia Yacht Squadron kept boats in place, but at least a dozen owners who moored their boats out in the Arm weren't so lucky. Yachts either broke free of their moorings or dragged them toward the Armdale Rotary. Some travelled almost a kilometre before crashing onto shore or into a wharf, with three ending up on Horseshoe Island and one jumping the retaining wall at Dingle park, coming to rest in the branches of a downed tree.

Some of the city's most expensive homes had boathouses sunk or floating docks thrown up on shore.

"Never saw nothing like it in my life," said Ray Blondell, a fisherman from Clarenville, Nfld., visiting his son in Halifax. "The tides were just unreal."

Many people cleaning up were heard to say it would be easier if only they could get a cup of coffee.

Some lined up at the few Tim Hortons with power, some used a barbecue to make coffee and some visited an impromptu coffee and tea stand on Windsor Street, where a pair of young entrepreneurs were charging $1 a cup.

—**Bill Spurr**

Men look at a jumble of debris in the middle of Agricola Street in Halifax early Monday.

DARREN PITTMAN

A walk through a strange, silent city

The air still smelled of sap when we left the house the morning after the hurricane.

Our house and all the other houses in the neighbourhood were covered with green confetti — leaves shredded and blown through the air with great force by Juan.

Our little dead-end street just north of Quinpool Road was a tangle of branches, trees and torn power lines. A power pole and a massive old elm had fallen onto a neighbour's roof. The pole pulled down the electrical mast from another neighbour's house, which yanked our mast away from the wall and pulled out some siding.

It was still raining a bit, and the sky was grey and gloomy.

We made coffee on the barbecue and commiserated with our neighbours for most of the morning. In the afternoon, we went for a walk.

A carpet of leaves and tangled branches covered the streets. All the buildings on Quinpool Road were dark.

At the Willow Tree intersection, cars were proceeding cautiously past the dead street lights.

On Cogswell, a piece of bright yellow vinyl siding was impaled on the rusted climbing spike of a power pole. The violence of the storm must have been astonishing.

There was water in the street and a jumble of trees near the wading pool on the Common.

We walked to the top of Citadel Hill and looked down at the strange, silent city. The sky was clearing, and the sun came out.

Barrington Street was a disturbing sight. The streets and sidewalks were covered with broken glass. Insulation panels and bits of plastic signs littered the street.

But workers were already busy repairing some windows.

At the ferry terminal, they were hammering planks to cover the empty spaces where glass

Barrington Street was disturbing on Monday.

PETER PARSONS

panels used to be. Insulation, bits of lumber and other debris floated in the water. A crowd of people stood around and watched.

It was about 2 p.m. now, and the boardwalk was filling up — a young, cheerful crowd, mostly students in shorts and T-shirts.

For them, with no property to worry about and no classes, it was a holiday. There was a strange carnival atmosphere with an undercurrent of anxiety.

We were getting hungry and tired.

How happy we were to find that the waterfront pub Stayner's Wharf was open!

The place was packed, some workers hadn't shown up and there was a line at the takeout window stretching around the block.

Still, within 30 minutes we had beer and good hot, simple food in front of us.

It was astonishing that they were serving lunch the day after the hurricane. I can't imagine how hard it must have been in the kitchen.

After lunch, we walked along and looked at the devastation on the waterfront — boardwalks, wharfs and boats smashed to matchsticks.

We walked past the Public Gardens, where giant trees had fallen, pulling up huge swaths of manicured lawn.

At Camp Hill Cemetery, a small pile of flowers marked the place where paramedic John Rossiter died while doing his job during the worst of the hurricane.

Jubilee Road was a tangle of fallen trees and power lines. Some of the side streets ended suddenly in a wall of greenery.

A young man with an axe on Jubilee Road was slowly trying to clear a huge deadfall across the street.

He swung inexpertly, taking breaks to catch his breath, but he was making headway through one trunk of the massive tree.

At times like this, we find out what we are made of.

We find that our neighbours will lend us propane when we need it to cook our supper.

We find that people will drive carefully and patiently through intersections that don't have traffic lights.

We find that young men will clear tangled brush in the rain without being asked.

We find that people will put up warning signs and hang reflector tape from dangerous wires.

We find that cooks and waitresses will work themselves ragged to feed hungry people when it really matters.

We find that we are made of something good.

—**Stephen Maher**

Craig Thompson laughs while he and his friend Tyler Mead pose for a photo for Joanne Shephard in front of a sign on a fallen power pole in Dartmouth.

TIM KROCHAK

The sea surge and high wind played havoc with fishermen's stages, wharfs and sheds, tearing apart this shed in Prospect.

For fishermen, absolute devastation

People in Prospect say it took hurricane Juan only moments to turn the seaside community, where many of them grew up, into something almost unrecognizable.

Almost three days after the winds died down, Ron Duggan stands at the end of the government wharf, the only one left upright, and gazes at the spot where his stage used to be.

He can point to the roof of his shed in the shattered shambles at the head of the cove. Sea surges put his two boats on the shore intact. But his 75 lobster traps were all swept into the water.

"The night of the storm, we were up till three o'clock trying to save things, but everything went in a hurry," he says. "It was there one minute, and the next minute it was all gone."

The loss won't ruin him, even with lobster season seven weeks away, but he's crestfallen.

Mr. Duggan started fishing for lobster at 13 and worked all the way through high school. He later joined the police force in Halifax but never gave up his lobster licence. He returned to Prospect before he retired and has been back fishing for the past 15 years. "It's in your blood — the ocean," says Mr. Duggan, 70.

Juan was the sort of storm people in the village heard their parents tell stories about.

"Dad used to have to put up with that sort of thing," Mr. Duggan says.

There used to be more wharfs and a cannery in the small cove, he says, and they likely prevented such severe damage.

"Now there's nothing left."

Looking at the jumbled pile of stages and sheds, Pam Christian points out which belonged to whom and where they used to stand.

"I'm really sad about it all because I grew up down here," she says.

"If it's not a direct relative of mine, it is of my husband, who's lost something here. We've looked at these all our lives, some of them. Now they're gone."

Three boats were damaged and two are still missing. One stage is turned around 180 degrees, and a shed is perched precariously over the water. Ms. Christian guesses an especially high tide will wash it away, too.

"I'm still a little shaky from it all," she said. "I don't know how we're going to clean it up."

Spirits are a bit higher along the coast at Peggys Cove.

The famous lighthouse weathered the storm unscathed. Some wharfs didn't fare well, but most homes seem undamaged.

The tourists lost no time taking in the sights. Hours after Juan moved on, they were pounding on the door of Beales' Bailiwick.

To reach it, they had to scale a pair of crumpled stairs, folded at strange angles when a channel of ocean water that poured over a seawall knocked the building housing the craft shop a half-metre forward.

"They were here first thing, knocking on the door, trying to get coffee. 'Is the store open? Can we come in anyway?' It's been awkward," says Tobias Beale, taking a break from trying to move the deck behind the building back into place.

But the demand is part of the reason he's working so hard to get things back in order.

"Everybody's anxious to get back to work," he says. "There are 15 people with jobs here, plus all the people making the crafts. There's $15,000 worth of sales lost from being closed."

Still, the men are in good cheer. At one point, Ben Stone comes up with a perch that's been washed under the deck.

Without a pause, John Beale Jr. remarks: "We've been looking everywhere for that."

—**John Gillis**

TIM KROCHAK / PHOTO OPPOSITE: TIM KROCHAK

Ed Glanville salvages a lobster trap from what was once a row of wharfs and fish shacks in Prospect. The community lost every one of its wharfs.

Two men row through the splintered remains of the wharfs of Herring Cove on Monday. The cove was a disaster area, with wharfs, stages and sheds all destroyed.

TIM KROCHAK

John Beale holds up a perch his friend, Ben Stone, found as the men were cleaning up behind Mr. Beale's parents' home in Peggys Cove.

TIM KROCHAK

Heartbreaking damage on the farm

John Dillman has left his Halifax County home countless times over the past 26 years to help fellow farmers in times of distress.

While that kindness has been returned tenfold to the Elderbank farmer and his family, this "catastrophe" requires more than the customary community rally of support.

"Somebody has got to wade in here with us on this one," said Mr. Dillman, whose Musqie Valley Farms was one of many devastated by hurricane Juan.

His dairy and beef barns were torn to shreds.

The family knew it was bad even as the storm howled the night of Sept. 28-29.

"We didn't let anyone out of the house until about 4 a.m., then we went out with flashlights to see what we were up against," Mr. Dillman said.

They knew a barn had come down because they heard the crash just before 1:30 a.m.

But daybreak revealed the scope of the devastation "this monster put on my family."

"We've been here 26 years and we got up ... in a position to start over," a shaken Mr. Dillman said.

Trapped cattle were freed from the wreckage of two barns and were on trucks to neighbouring farms by 6 a.m.

The storm spawned some form of mini-tornado that scratched a path in the earth between his dairy barn and son Reg's beef barn.

The same path of destruction cut through the woods in a straight line to the Fox family's goat farm, which was also levelled.

Mr. Dillman said community support has been superb, with the Archibald family at Hill Peak Farms and the Holman family at Scotiaview Farms taking in his dairy herd.

The Gladwin family took in his young cattle, while the beef herd remains in the pasture.

"It's awful hard to see them walk in your driveway to help you. We're not sitting here crying in

John Dillman stands in front of a flattened building on his farm near Elderbank. He lost two barns.

our soup."

He says it's a crime that some families may be forced from generations of farming by a storm.

But without wind insurance on his buildings and with both levels of government vowing only to speed up the disaster relief process, Mr. Dillman says he needs more than the helping hands of his neighbours to clean up and rebuild.

"There are a lot of reasons for deciding to leave an industry; don't let Juan be the reason for it. I don't want this storm to win. But you feel like you're out there on your own."

He says farmers must decide quickly whether to put up expensive new barns or to rent space to house herds.

Others face huge cleanup bills and lost buildings that stored feed. He estimates his bill will be about $300,000.

"We might be 10 years coming out of this ... to get back to where we were" the morning of Sept. 28, he said.

And that's if they can even afford to get started on the comeback trail.

—**Barry Dorey**

A lone stalk of corn remains standing in a field flattened by Juan near Middle Musquodoboit.

In parks and woods, arboreal carnage

"This is quite possibly the worst damage to our urban canopy since the Halifax Explosion. It's that significant and that order of magnitude."

Mike Labrecque, director of real property and asset management for Halifax Regional Municipality, made that statement the day after hurricane Juan blew into town, uprooting thousands of trees and closing 600 parks.

Point Pleasant Park, with its Norway spruce and Scottish fir and pine, its slender birches and willows, was almost wiped out by the hurricane, whose devastation Mayor Peter Kelly described as "astronomical."

Point Pleasant lost half to two-thirds of its trees, the mayor said after a helicopter tour of the 75-hectare park—a loss unprecedented in its history, which dates back to 1866.

And the venerable, much-loved Public Gardens lost 20 per cent of its trees and many of its flowers. The Gardens were locked to visitors, and it was weeks before any other parks reopened in the City of Trees, as Halifax has fondly been called.

People were asked to stay away from the parks to give cleanup crews a chance to start clearing and replanting.

"It's a mess in there," Dave Large of the municipal parks department said of Point Pleasant. "Hundreds of trees have come down."

David Shaw, who lives near the park, said he could hear trees snapping from inside his house as the hurricane raged. "It sounded terrible."

The municipality will have to start a reforestation program, the mayor said. "It will take generations to get it back to what it once was."

George McLellan, chief administrative officer of the municipality, said it broke his heart to see the destruction in the park.

"It underscores the power of the storm, and that really goes to the heart of the effort that we need to undertake to restore the city to normal," he said.

People have already approached the municipality to start a rebuilding campaign in local parks.

For Councillor Dawn Sloane, the sight of the Public Gardens' uprooted century-old trees just after Juan petered out was hard to take. "It's a traumatic experience we went through."

Apparently, many passersby felt the same way. For days after the hurricane, hundreds of people stood gazing in at the destruction from outside the park gates.

A similar scene was played out at Flynn Park, off lower Quinpool Road in the city's west end.

Two or three dozen trees were either toppled, damaged or hauled out by the roots, said Councillor Sheila Fougere.

"Tree after tree after tree, it's just like a giant domino game."

Outside Halifax, the sad tale was much the same, as hundreds of woodland owners in central Nova Scotia struggled to salvage what they could in jumbles of downed trees.

From Halifax County to Pictou County, Juan uprooted countless thousands of trees worth millions of dollars. Jacqueline May of the Nova Scotia Forest Alliance, in Stewiacke, said woodland owners lost up to 70 per cent of their trees.

"It is a sight few people have ever witnessed," said Hants County woodland owner Earle Tanner, who owns 200 hectares near Shubenacadie. "It's impossible to measure all the forest destruction in the area."

Added Donald Parker of Middle Musquodoboit, who lost most of the trees on his 200-hectare site: "The devastation to woodlands will still be visible and felt by Nova Scotia landowners and wildlife for 20 to 30 years."

—Amy Pugsley Fraser and Bill Power

TIM KROCHAK / PHOTO OPPOSITE: ERIC WYNNE

Above: For a week after Juan, Nova Scotia was a wonderland for children: no school and loads of dead trees to play on. Mathieu Bornais and Devon McKay, both 12, scaled this giant in Leighton Dillman Park in Dartmouth on Tuesday.

Facing page: Point Pleasant Park took the brunt of Juan, losing hundreds of trees in a few hours, as this aerial photo shows.

TED PRITCHARD

A steady stream of Haligonians came to the gates of the Public Gardens to have a look at the devastation inside. The park lost 20 per cent of its trees.

Where once there stood a forest, Juan left a tangle of deadfalls. Nothing in history, not even the Halifax Explosion, damaged Point Pleasant Park as badly as Juan.

A massive hardwood toppled by hurricane Juan fell out of the Public Gardens, smashing the wrought-iron fence, and ended up with its crown in Summer Street.

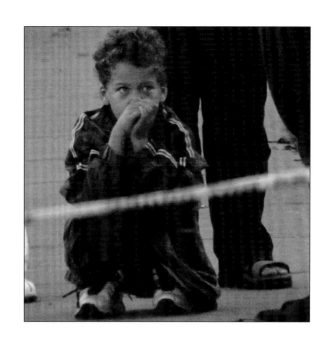

Tragedy

Falling trees take two lives

Just a few hours before hurricane Juan struck, John Michael Rossiter put in a call to his parents in Newfoundland.

"I'm at work right now and something really exciting is happening here in Halifax," said the 31-year-old paramedic.

"John, be safe," Bill Rossiter warned his son.

"You were in this business 30 years, and you were OK," John replied.

But tragedy struck just after 1 a.m., Sept. 29. As the fierce wind gathered force, a 20-metre tree came crashing down, crushing the rear end of the ambulance in which Mr. Rossiter was riding.

He was killed instantly.

At almost the same moment, Stephen Donald Munro, 50, of Upper Burlington, Hants County, was killed on Highway 14 in Nine Mile River after his vehicle was hit by a falling tree.

He was on his way home from IMP Aerospace, where he had worked for seven years.

Mr. Munro had served in the Canadian Armed Forces for 24 years before starting at IMP.

He was born in Windsor, son of Arthur Robert Munro and the late Jean B. (Davies) Munro.

Mr. Munro is survived by his wife, Shirley, and three daughters, Annette, Elizabeth and Stephanie, plus grandchildren.

His funeral was held Oct. 2.

Mr. Rossiter, born in Mount Pearl, Nfld., had worked as a paramedic in the Halifax area for about 10 years.

"He became a paramedic partly because it was in the family and partly because he wanted to help people," said his sister, Karen Rossiter.

His elder brother was a paramedic, then went on to become a police officer. His father is a retired deputy fire chief.

Ms. Rossiter said her brother, who was single and devoted to his relatives, loved people—"a typical Newfoundlander."

Colleagues and members of the public set up a makeshift memorial at the place where John Michael Rossiter was killed during hurricane Juan.

A member of the Nova Scotia Government and General Employees Union, Local 42, he led co-workers through the 18-hour strike in 1999 and helped pen the first unionized contract for paramedics under one employer, Emergency Medical Care Inc.

"We will never forget the contribution he made to this union or his dedication to protecting the rights of all paramedics in this province," said NSGEU president Joan Jessome.

The day after his death, the Rossiter family visited Province House, where MLAs honoured him with a moment of silence.

"John Rossiter lived as a hero and will be remembered as a hero, first by his family, but also by Nova Scotians, by Newfoundlanders and by all Canadians who remember those who have lost their lives in the line of duty," Premier John Hamm said.

A shrine to Mr. Rossiter has been set up at the accident site, in the heart of downtown Halifax. A paramedic's reflective vest hangs from a wrought-iron stake, part of the Camp Hill Cemetery fence that was toppled by uprooted and fallen trees.

Nearby, amid broken glass, lie two flashlights, flowers and four paramedic badges. A figurine of a paramedic carrying a medical bag stands among the relics.

In marker pen, people have written tributes to Mr. Rossiter on what looks like vinyl upholstery from a vehicle.

"You were taken too early for all you have done," says one. "You will be missed more than words can express. RIP."

Robert Boudreau of Antigonish, Mr. Rossiter's partner on the job for almost four years, said he "died doing what he loved to do."

"He was a very good paramedic, very career-oriented. He performed at the top of his class."

Mr. Boudreau recalled an exchange with a supervisor.

"He said, 'We lost a good paramedic today.' I looked at him and said, 'You lost three good paramedics when you lost John.' "

His funeral was Oct. 1.

—Jennifer Stewart and Cathy von Kintzel

Health-care workers who knew John Michael Rossiter left notes at his memorial. 'You will be missed more than words can express,' wrote one.

PETER PARSONS

'Mary is gone to make flowers'

TIM KROCHAK

Friends and neighbours are disconsolate after learning of the deaths of Mary Sack and her two children.

Many people broke down in tears recounting the early-morning fire that killed a mother and two of her children in west-end Halifax.

Frank Janes was at his father's house on Chisholm Avenue when he saw flames rip through a townhouse at 3494 Micmac St. just before 12:50 a.m. on Sept. 30.

It was only a day after hurricane Juan swept through, knocking out power all over the city. Firefighters believe the fire was started by a candle.

Mr. Janes raced over and began kicking in the front door. Others used toys from the front yard and cans of pop to smash in a front window.

"We booted the door in ... and the flames just shot out through," Mr. Janes said. "There was nothing you could do. We tried, but we ... "

His voice trailed off as tears started to flow.

Neighbours frantically tried to wake Mary Sack, her husband, Billy Amro, and their three children, Anna, 5, Zachary, 4, and Samia, 2.

"I was kicking the door and Frankie was kicking the door," Melissa Allison said. "I was yelling, 'Billy, Mary, get out! There's a fire!' "

Only Mr. Amro awoke. Clad in his underwear, he jumped out onto a small pitched roof just below an upstairs window.

But realizing his family was still inside, he went back and managed to rescue Anna.

Others also tried to go back inside. But in only a couple of minutes, the blaze was already out of control.

"All I know is, Billy was yelling for his wife and kids. He was freaking out really bad," Ms. Allison said. "He was just yelling: 'My kids! My kids! Mary!' "

Despite their valiant efforts, many blamed themselves for being unable to rescue Ms. Sack, Zachary and Samia.

"We couldn't save all of them, but we could save two," Ms. Allison said, fighting back tears.

Mr. Amro handed Anna down to neighbours Kevin Dillman and Sean Tucker, both of whom later had difficulty describing the little girl's struggle to breathe.

"I was just trying to keep her focused on me and praying with her and trying to keep her away from all the screaming at the time," Mr. Tucker said.

When firefighters arrived, the townhouse was engulfed.

They searched the building for the three trapped occupants and found one child.

They performed CPR without success.

Many children watched as fire and police investigators combed through the wreckage; all but one upstairs room was gutted.

One child asked a neighbour when Ms. Sack, 23, a friend to all the local kids, was coming back.

"Mary is gone to make flowers—God needs her up there to work in His garden," Sheila Westhaver told the girl.

Neighbours agreed Ms. Sack's home was a favourite meeting place for kids.

"They got along with everybody," Mr. Janes said. "All the kids around here, that's where they used to go."

Ms. Sack grew up on the Indian Brook reserve, near Shubenacadie. Mr. Amro, originally from Palestine, was taking classes to become a certified mechanic.

In the aftermath of the hurricane, firefighters responded to four other candle-related fires.

Some said Ms. Sack, Zachary and Samia wouldn't have died had battery-operated smoke detectors been used in the public housing units rather than the electric ones that don't work when the power is out.

—Randy Jones

Coping

Born in the teeth of a gale

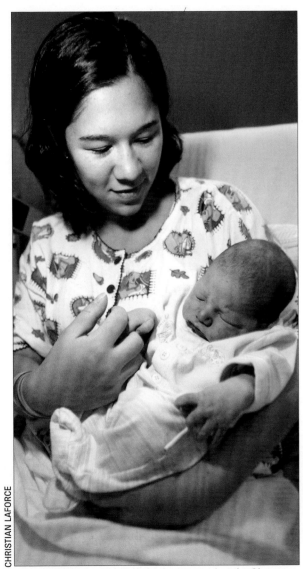

CHRISTIAN LAFORCE

Crystal Cheung holds little Cameron Austin Cheung, who was born at the IWK during hurricane Juan.

In the eerie calm that settled over Halifax just after the fury of hurricane Juan abated, a new life took its first breath.

It was 3:27 a.m., Sept. 29, when Cameron Austin Cheung was born at the IWK Health Centre, weighing in at eight pounds six ounces.

By that time, the hurricane was bearing down on Prince Edward Island.

Crystal Cheung of Halifax was just as glad that Cameron waited for the worst of the storm to pass before making his entrance into the world.

On the other hand, the hurricane did make for an interesting labour, said Ms. Cheung, 21.

"There will certainly be stories to tell him when he is old enough to understand," she said with a smile.

Ms. Cheung arrived at the health centre in south-end Halifax hours before the storm struck.

She said she was more preoccupied with her own situation than the magnitude of what was happening outside. A hospital room television advised her and other expectant mothers that the hurricane would hit Halifax soon.

As her labour intensified, so did the force of Juan.

At 12:15 a.m., Sept. 29, the hurricane made landfall, between Prospect and Shad Bay.

Soon it was pummelling the Halifax area.

"Even in the darkness you could see the wind and the rain whipping everything around and putting down trees .... There was also lightning ... and every so often, something would bang into the window," Ms. Cheung remembered two days later, as sunshine streamed into her room.

Ms. Cheung said staff at the hospital remained reassuringly calm as the hurricane howled outside, even though many of them were probably very anxious about how their own families were doing.

"Some of the staff must have been worried about what was happening at their own homes," she said.

Ms. Cheung received an epidural anesthetic, making her final hours of labour relatively comfortable despite the hurricane's violent disruption of Halifax's south end.

Sighs of relief echoed through the ward as the hurricane headed inland, she said.

It was at this moment of relative peace that Ms. Cheung gave birth to her first baby.

She said she likes the timing of his birth, in the calm just after the storm.

"I'm saving the news clippings for my son for when he is older," she said.

Ms. Cheung said she considered but dismissed suggestions she name her son after the hurricane.

"I thought about it," she said. But she decided to stick with her choice, Cameron Austin.

Hospital officials could not confirm the exact number but estimated that more than a dozen babies were born in the hours before and immediately after Juan hit town.

"All maternity services were operating as normal the day of and the day after the hurricane," health centre spokeswoman Naomi Shelton said.

She said the centre was unable to say whether any of the babies were named Juan.

—Bill Power

A reminder to live life to the fullest

It must be the lucky scar. The one above Edith Benoit's left eye. Her unique reminder of the Halifax Explosion—and of 85 years of remarkable survival.

From Dec. 6, 1917, to Sept. 29, 2003—from the explosion to hurricane Juan, and many points in between—Mrs. Benoit, 87, has been through it all. And emerged to tell the tale.

At her home on Atlantic Street in Halifax's south end three days after the hurricane, Mrs. Benoit took stock of her latest brush with disaster.

"I did take a tumble in the dark," she said of losing power in her house.

But even her lights came on more quickly than those in neighbouring homes—and as for damage, just one tree in the backyard came down.

Other than that, the tidy home where she's lived for 43 years escaped Juan without a scratch.

And this in a neighbourhood where many properties were devastated, where nearby Point Pleasant Park lost so many trees that its remains have been described as a wasteland. Mrs. Benoit just figures her lucky scar came through again.

It all began when she was only a year old, in 1917, in the Halifax Explosion.

"My parents thought I was dead. They found me on a stretcher at the Halifax Commons with the rest of the survivors. My face was all covered in blood."

Miraculously, she came through the disaster with only the one scar.

True, that scar was something of an embarrassment—especially for the 14-year-old who found herself huddled atop Citadel Hill with thousands of other Haligonians in 1945, after a series of explosions at the Bedford Magazine threatened to remove the city from the map.

"I'm thinking to myself: 'Why me, Lord?'" she recalls.

It was at that moment—having survived her second disaster—that she decided the scar above her eye had to be lucky, a reminder to live life to the fullest.

Despite the limitations of the walker that Mrs. Benoit uses to get around, she remains exceptionally active—even asking a visitor if a spot of ballroom dancing might be in order.

Her modest home is filled with certificates of appreciation from the federal and provincial governments and community organizations for her many years of volunteer work.

She's affectionately called Sarge by many friends and admirers who knew her as sergeant-at-arms with the Scotia branch of the Royal Canadian Legion.

Matter of fact, that's what her friends shouted to her on the night of Aug. 7, 2003, after a powerful explosion rocked the waterfront grain elevator near her neighbourhood.

"They were pounding on the door and yelling, 'Sarge! Sarge! You've got to get out of here!'" the diminutive woman recalls.

That night, she and about 400 other south-end residents were evacuated from their homes.

Officers from Halifax Regional Police helped get her to safety—and Mrs. Benoit added yet another page to her disaster survival file.

And then came Juan.

After all this, Mrs. Benoit figures she was destined to be a survivor.

That injury, back in 1917, could have meant the loss of her eye—or worse, she says.

"I was the lucky one."

—Bill Power

TED PRITCHARD

Halifax Explosion survivor Edith Benoit watches hurricane cleanup work from her front door.

Gregory Higden, 8, walks with his lantern up Westbrook Avenue in Dartmouth, as his father and their dog Sascha follow in front of headlights late Monday.

'This brought out the best in us'

Sometimes bad things bring out the best in people—and that's what happened across Nova Scotia in the difficult days after Juan.

Nadine McNamara of Dartmouth got up at 4:30 a.m. two mornings in a row to build a community firepit. People came to cook, share food and enjoy the company.

"I have children and grandchildren and this is very scary for everybody," she said. "Kids need comfort, and this has been done since time immemorial — people gathering together to share conversation, food and company."

Many didn't have a lot but feasted on pooled resources. It was particularly poignant for this to happen in a low-income area that's more often in the news because of crime.

"We may be poor, but this brought out the best in us," Ms. McNamara said.

"It's about people helping people."

She and neighbour Pat Ryan first got a makeshift barbecue going Monday and combined their food for a potluck stew — some soup, some hamburger, a big pot, and soon there was enough to feed a few families.

"It was a big stew — we fed about 12 people," Mrs. Ryan said.

At supper, they built an open-pit fire and put on coffee and tea for anybody in the area.

"I had hamburgers, and I said, 'If you want to put anything on it, just bring a pan, the meat and cook it,' " Mrs. Ryan said.

Fifteen people gathered for a campfire that turned from dinner to an evening of good company. "We were all out there wishing we had marshmallows," a beaming Mrs. Ryan said.

Ms. McNamara rose early and stoked the embers for a breakfast of bacon, eggs and toast, complete with coffee and tea.

They were out of some basics, but neighbours brought over instant coffee, sugar and tea bags.

TIM KROCHAK / PHOTO OPPOSITE: TIM KROCHAK

Moe Lavoie and other tenants of the Northbrook apartment building in Dartmouth made the most of the first night without power, smoking, chatting and having a few beers by candlelight on their front steps.

It was much the same story for neighbours a few blocks over from Ms. McNamara.

"Some of the food was going soft on us, so we decided we might as well all share the food," Andrea Simms recalled.

With six apartments in her building, they dined on steak, chicken and scalloped potatoes.

The neighbours sat around a plastic picnic table with a few candles and a few drinks and enjoyed the warm evening.

"You might as well get together with people as sit alone in the dark," she said.

Many of the neighbours had worked side by side all day, clearing downed trees.

Andrew Karanfilis enjoyed relaxing with friends by candlelight. "I find electricity takes away from the human spirit," he said.

He said he minimizes his use of electricity and often relies on candles anyway.

"It took a natural disaster for all of us to get together and finally have a barbecue," he said.

—Beverley Ware

Hungry for power, with no excuse

I first started feeling it in my stomach on Day 2. Mixed in with hunger pangs were the inklings of anxiety.

My phone was still out. So was the power. And from what I had seen of Halifax since hurricane Juan clobbered us, the prospect of things returning to normal quickly seemed more remote than it did early on.

My cupboard was bare. Let me rephrase that: It was stocked with food I couldn't cook, and the dregs in the fridge were getting less appetizing by the day.

I wasn't ready. And I had no excuse.

It's not as if I didn't know hurricane Juan was going to smash us in the face.

I'm the guy who did the front page of The Sunday Herald for Sept. 28. I'm the guy who wrote the biggest headline that space would allow in order to warn everybody else. After my shift was done, I distinctly remember getting on the phone to my girlfriend to impress upon her the seriousness of the matter.

She was skeptical. Hurricanes always peter out before they hit Nova Scotia, she said.

Deep down, that's what I must have believed, too. I should have known better.

A decade ago, I saw with my own eyes the devastation hurricane Andrew had wrought in south Florida.

Granted, Juan couldn't hold a candle to Andrew.

It wasn't just the wholesale massacre of trees in Florida that stuck in my mind, but the sight of eviscerated buildings with their roofs ripped off and their contents scattered to the four winds. Weeks later, the U.S. National Guard was still in command of the streets.

That was the only time I can recall engaging in the somewhat shameless pastime of "disaster tourism."

Until the morning after Juan in Halifax.

I was free of cleanup duty, so, like many other Haligonians, I had the luxury of wandering around the neighbourhood to assess the damage to other people's property. (My condo building came through the storm just fine — although the magnificent maritime pines I loved to gaze upon from my window were mercilessly beheaded.)

What I saw in my immediate vicinity shocked me. Not because I had never seen anything like it — I had — but because these were intimately familiar places that had been torn apart.

Stately trees had been shoved like battering rams into stately homes. One sailboat had been tossed ashore, discarded like a toy after a child's attention suddenly wanders elsewhere. The park I visit to unwind had become an obstacle course, with felled trunks blocking the paths.

The novelty of disaster tourism quickly wore off. As the day progressed, I got a hankering to make myself useful in some vague way. Specifically, I wanted to go downtown to visit my parents, who live in a condo building. But I was trapped — the Armdale Rotary had been sealed off to traffic. I knew my parents were OK — a kind neighbour had let me use his phone — but I still wanted to see them.

It was dark by the time I navigated my way there, through traffic jams and spooky avenues devoid of the comforting halo of street lights and still awash with the flotsam and jetsam of Juan's passing.

I think it was while I was clambering up eight floors in a pitch-black stairwell to get to my parents' door that I realized I had missed my chance to make myself useful — by a long shot.

I had no supplies to bring them, just my dubious company. And I feared I had no reasonable prospect of restocking them, much less myelf, for several more days.

Thankfully, my mother takes the weather channel more seriously than I do. She had boiled some rice in anticipation of a power outage and had planned several meals of cold cuts.

She just hadn't expected the electricity to be out this long, so even she would soon run out of food. The stores in her neighbourhood still weren't open 48 hours after the storm.

In the end, I knew we'd get by. Some restaurants were open downtown. And I had many friends with barbecues and food that had to be eaten lest it went bad. (Being a single guy who doesn't really relish eating alone, I have honed my charming personality to the point where I am quite expert at bumming meals from a rather extensive network of people at the best of times.)

Better yet, I had the means to get either the food to my family or my family to the food.

You see, I did get one thing right in terms of preparedness.

Surprisingly, it dawned on me that I should fill up the car before the hurricane hit. So I wasn't starved for gas, like many other motorists I'd seen out there besieging that last station with its lights on.

In the dark of night, with only the cat and the radio for company, I came to the realization that it wasn't the lack of power that bugged me. It was the powerlessness. And the knowledge I could have done something about it.

If I had to grade my initial performance, I'd give myself a D. For dumb.

But that might not be the final verdict. I knew true failure would come if I had to crack open that can of Ensure I buried in my cupboard. It was a liquid meal replacement I bought a while back to get me through gum surgery.

I never stooped that low, but on Day 2 it was looking pretty good.

—**Laurent Le Pierres**

A struggle to feed the hungry

ERIC WYNNE

Peter Bennett of Dartmouth makes a face as he empties some spoiled food into the green bin.

Many Nova Scotians were hungry and in need of emergency supplies after hurricane Juan.

"We have no money to buy food — we're not rich, we can't just go out and buy it," said Eileen Bowser, who lives in Halifax's Sunrise Manor, public housing for seniors.

Up the street at Ahearn Manor, hundreds of seniors and families also had little food.

The Red Cross dropped off water, juice and granola bars in the dark lobby, but residents had to come down and get the food or wait for others to take it to them.

Betty Thomas, a diabetic, was worried. "I haven't taken my insulin," she said. "It's in the fridge, but it's warm. I don't know if it's any good."

Natasha Jackson of the regional housing authority said staff were trying to help nearly 5,000 seniors and 5,000 low-income families — without power or phones in the office.

Kathy Barbour, a personal-care worker with Northwood Homecare, was visiting seniors.

"They want to know what's going on," she said. "Some can't even see out the window, but they're accepting it very well."

Some were getting frustrated.

After days without power, Laura Parnell of Halifax found her food was ruined, and she didn't have money to buy more for her kids, aged 16, 14 and 12. "I'm on a budget, I'm on family benefits."

But help did arrive.

Staff from the province's Community Services Department worked out of the Red Cross call centre and helped deliver food.

Red Cross general manager John Byrne said that as of Oct. 2, the Red Cross had helped 20,000 people affected by the storm.

Superstore, Sobeys and Costco Wholesale provided food, and firms like M&M Meats, Canadian Tire and Tim Hortons also made donations.

The day after the storm, the Red Cross took supplies to hundreds of people in more than a dozen seniors and family public housing complexes, from Mount Uniacke to Musquodoboit Harbour. The Red Cross also teamed up with the Metro Food Bank Society-Nova Scotia to send a food truck to the Truro area.

Halifax-area food banks were getting a lot of calls from people who couldn't afford to replace food lost because of power outages, said Dianne Swinemar, executive director of the Metro Food Bank Society-Nova Scotia.

Most of the 40 Halifax-area food banks were back on track by Oct. 1, but shelves emptied fast.

A week after the hurricane, the society was seeking help itself.

Several corporations stepped in to help. ReMax Nova, metro's largest real estate firm, raised over $4,000 in hours.

Aliant Mobility organized a food drive for the agency, and Mic Mac Mall challenged Halifax Shopping Centre to see which mall could collect the most food.

At the Kent hardware store in Halifax's Bayers Lake, managers opened early the morning after Juan and led customers around with flashlights to buy emergency supplies.

The Home Depot in Dartmouth opened at 5 a.m. to serve customers lined up outside.

Nubody's in Halifax cut its day rate to $5 from $10, so people could have hot showers.

Irving gas stations supplied free muffins, juice and water.

And in Petite Riviere, near Bridgewater, Happy Haven Seniors Home offered seniors free room and board — and a ride to and from Halifax, if needed.

—John Gillis, Eva Hoare, Clare Mellor, Steve Proctor, Jennifer Stewart and Beverley Ware

Milk (and bacon) of human kindness

Bacon and eggs were flying off the barbecue outside the Ardmore Tea Room on Quinpool Road just two days after hurricane Juan.

When staff at the 51-year-old Halifax restaurant realized the power wasn't coming on any time soon, they agreed to cook up what would spoil and feed the neighbourhood for free.

"We decided that instead of throwing it out, we should just give it away," said owner Darrell Cormier.

The Ardmore staff and a host of volunteers first broke out the grills the day after the storm, serving up everything from scallops and salmon to hamburgers and chicken fingers. About 2,000 people came by to dine.

The cooks called it quits only when it became too dark to see the food on people's plates.

"We cooked 500 sausages in an hour," head cook Gilbert Warren said. "We had flames three feet high on the barbecue. It was insane."

People lined up as far back as the Tim Hortons a block away in anticipation of the free buffet.

"It's awesome," said Melissa Steele, holding a paper plate piled high with scrambled eggs, bacon and a toasted English muffin.

The 22-year-old Dalhousie student had coped by barbecuing with friends the first few days.

"I just live across the street and I had nothing to eat, so I came over to grab a bite," she said.

While some came for the meals, others dropped by to lend a hand.

Chelsey Thompson, one of the Ardmore's regular customers, spent the day in a dark corner slicing English muffins.

"I think it's a great idea," Mr. Thompson said.

"I'm not doing anything at home and there's nothing to watch on TV, so I said, 'I'll come over and help them.' "

—Jennifer Stewart

CHRISTIAN LAFORCE

Sylvain Bourgeois makes coffee in front of the Ardmore Tea Room. The restaurant fed the neighbourhood for free.

When the going gets tough ...

Nova Scotians found ingenious ways to cope after hurricane Juan left them in the dark for a second day — and a third.

Some decided to pack it in and pack up rather than face another cold shower.

For Deanna and Blair Landry of Halifax, that meant P.E.I.

Mr. Landry had to convince his wife they should buy a barbecue with a side burner this summer, and now he dubbed himself a genius as he boiled water for coffee. Their supper hot off the grill was fun the night before, too.

But the Landrys and their children — six, three and 18 months — were looking forward to a few creature comforts at Grandma's house.

"We're going to bring our laundry over, just like I'm back in university," Mrs. Landry said.

Neighbourhood children took advantage of gorgeous early fall weather to play in backyards during the first two days of the power outage, but the number of children around was dwindling.

"A lot of their friends have gone as well," Mrs. Landry said. "One of our neighbours packed up his kids and took them to the Sheraton."

In Tantallon, Steve and Carrie Edwards decided two nights with an excited toddler running around in a pitch-black house was enough.

"We couldn't keep track of him in the dark," Ms. Edwards said of 18-month-old Sam, who along with his father left for his grandfather's in Hantsport.

"I said to Steve, 'You should go,' " she said. 'You go and have a shower.' "

Those who didn't leave town sopped up water leaking from defrosting fridges and spent another day on the protein diet, barbecuing meat before it went bad.

Corinne Abraham of Clearview Drive in Bedford got electricity late the day after the storm, so she was able to phone the families of

CHRISTIAN LAFORCE

SOME TOUGH IT OUT: People line up for propane at a gas station two days after the hurricane.

the kids she looks after in her home, telling them it was OK to bring back the kids.

"Even if it just gives the parents an opportunity to go and get a shower somewhere, because some of them are on pumps and have no water or electricity or phone," she said. "So I was leaving messages on their phone and they would use their cellphone to get their message to find out, 'Oh my God, Corinne has power and I can leave my kid there.' So they went and stood in line to get milk and stuff and anything they could to straighten out their own lives."

At workplaces downtown, where there was power, people brought their kids to work for a shower or had a cold shower at home and took a hair dryer to work.

In Hatchet Lake, a man whose well didn't work

because of the power outage bathed in the lake and fetched water in buckets to flush the toilet.

The impact of Juan was felt even in places that didn't lose power, like Windsor Home Hardware.

"It's just nuts, all of metro has been here since 10 yesterday morning," owner Jeff Redden said.

"Flashlights, batteries, coolers, radios, butane cooking stoves .... The RCMP bought 150 packs of D batteries to take back to the city. We sent to the warehouse in Debert for a truckload of stuff and people are waiting around for that truck to get here, and if we had any chainsaws or generators left, we could have sold 100 of each.

"People are also lined up at the Irving for gas and propane and taking advantage of the chance to go to Tim Hortons while they're in town."

—**Bill Spurr**

SOME HEAD FOR GRANDMA'S: Motorists from across the city lined up for gasoline at this station in Lower Sackville, one of the few left open on Monday.

After Juan, generosity of spirit

Hurricane Juan showed Nova Scotians that true power doesn't come from electrical wires, but from kindness and generosity to others at a time of urgent need.

The devastation was undeniable. But destruction is not the only theme of the storm. In e-mails to The Herald, readers wrote that in Juan's aftermath, their neighbours stood tall.

They wrote about friends and strangers who helped clear yards, shared power, delivered hot meals.

They wrote about a woman who delivered muffins to her neighbours on Halifax's Henry Street and businesses like the Cow Bay Road Irving station, which gave away muffins, granola bars and bottles of water and juice.

"The residents of the HRM are spectacular people who care about each other and their city," wrote Candace Salmon.

"While I felt immense sorrow at the loss of much of our waterfront and Public Gardens, as well as homes and foliage, those things are reparable. We are so blessed to have not lost more lives, for those are the things Halifax could not replace.

"As for the workers who are trying to repair our city, thank you. And for those of us who are left to wait, let us be thankful we have each other."

Writers also told us of those who shared generators and freezers so their neighbours wouldn't have to throw away food.

David Carlson praised his brother-in-law, Peter Stewart of River John.

"If it wasn't for his willingness to share his generator, many of us would be throwing out hundreds of dollars worth of food from our deep-freezers. Peter would hook up his generator long enough to prevent our fridge or freezer from thawing out before he would move it on to some-one else who needed to keep things cold. He would also keep the generator topped up with gas purchased with money out of his own pocket."

In Halifax's south end, Catherine and Mike Ritchie were praised for sharing their generator with everyone on their block.

"Every family gets it for four hours a day in two-hour shifts, and three families plug in at once .... Not only have (they) shared their generator, but he had done up a schedule for use and given himself the worst time slot," wrote Linda Keddy.

At Fort Massey United Church in Halifax, families without power congregated at the church, which did have power, to cook chowder, pastas and stews. The food went to neighbours who had no way to cook.

Alan Benninger wrote that he had gone to the church to donate food, "but this has been a wonderful experience to have been a part of, and it's really the minister, his family and other members of the church who are the real ones to thank for such a nice Good Samaritan story."

Cristal Arnold wrote about her parents, Debbie and Wally Arnold of Lower Sackville, who used their camping stove and barbecue to make hot drinks for neighbours and helped clear their yards of debris. When their power came back on, they opened their home to neighbours still without it, offering hot food and hot showers to anyone who needed them.

"They are the best, and I am glad they are my parents," she wrote.

Crissy Richardson wrote to laud the entire community of Minesville, which was struggling with overwhelming damage to property, tangles of trees and power poles downed like toothpicks.

"People who received damage to their homes or required assistance were identified, and groups of volunteers responded .... Community members organized the rental of a freezer.... One day our community will be beautiful again, but our sense of community and togetherness is shining through now."

Some acts of kindness were for people too far away to offer help. Paula Slauenwhite of Oakville, Ont., was desperately worried about her brother Buddy and his family in Herring Cove.

"I read your paper online and when I read: 'Damage to Herring Cove is extreme,' I totally panicked. Power was out, phone lines were down and I felt totally helpless. I sent an e-mail to every Maritimer I knew, hoping to hear some tidbit of information that would put my mind at ease."

Suzanne Owens and her colleague Jocelyn Smith, who live not far from her brother's street, came to the rescue. Ms. Smith offered to drive by to take a look.

"This morning I received an e-mail that informed me that my brother's house was intact, the big tree in the front yard was still standing," Slauenwhite wrote. "No power, but they were OK. What a huge relief."

Hope, of course, blooms eternal.

When Judy MacDonald sold her house in New Brunswick four years ago, she asked the new owners if she could transplant a rose bush her children had given her for Mother's Day to her new home in Halifax.

It flourished, growing to about two metres tall.

The morning of Sept. 29, she had some help cleaning up her demolished yard.

"Two neighbours helped me secure the rose bush, hoping the slightly raised roots would re-anchor. Yesterday, as I was continuing to gather twigs and bundle them, I noticed a bloom on my rose bush. It hasn't bloomed for weeks, yet yesterday a full flower had opened its petals, symbolizing renewal, hope and forgiveness."

—Kelly Shiers

Paul Archer, Simon Jones and Bryan Jordan haul branches from a backyard in Halifax. Saint Mary's University football players helped clear senior citizens' yards.

'My mom said we'd better pray'

Few would have wanted to walk a mile in Anne Macdonald's shoes as she waded through antiques and personal belongings sucked from her home and strewn around her yard by hurricane Juan's destructive forces.

She and her elderly parents, Ruth and Allan Macdonald, huddled together on their couch praying in the early morning hours of Sept. 29 as their large barn, filled with machinery, was flattened and the roof was ripped from a two-storey section of their hilltop house in Cooks Brook, Halifax County.

She couldn't say why her family stayed downstairs in a one-storey addition to the house that stormy night instead of sleeping in their upstairs bedrooms that sustained unimaginable damage.

"We get strong winds on this hill at the best of times, and I just had a bad feeling," Ms. Macdonald said a week after the storm.

Ms. Macdonald vividly recalled the deafening roar of wind that filled the century-old house near Middle Musquodoboit, showing no mercy for her family's cherished belongings and memories. A trap door to the attic blew open, and the hurricane scattered antiques and debris throughout the upstairs. A window and frame were sucked out of the steel front door.

"My mom said we'd better pray, and that's what we did," she said. "We prayed to God that we'd survive the night."

They did survive, uninjured, along with their two traumatized cats, to face the devastation awaiting them upstairs and outside, where trees were toppled and pieces of house and barn were scattered around the yard.

Sections of two brick chimneys were blown many metres, embedding themselves in the ground. Worse yet, heavy rain later that morning drenched the roofless house, soaking walls, ceilings and floors.

Anne Macdonald walks by the flattened barn behind her family's Cooks Brook home.

"It was everything my parents worked for," Ms. Macdonald said, referring to her 85-year-old mother and 89-year-old father, who lived in the house all his life.

A contractor has started repairs, but the family probably won't be back in the house until Christmas. The three moved into a travel trailer on their property, equipped with a generator.

"The kindness that's been shown to us is overwhelming and humbling," she said, describing how friends and relatives filled their heavily damaged house by 7 a.m. on the morning of the storm and helped save hundreds of valuables still upstairs and scattered around the property.

A photo of her grandfather was found undamaged in alder bushes, looking as though it had been gently placed there. Later, Mr. Macdonald found a box of salvageable family photos.

In the aftermath, friends, neighbours and relatives threw an impromptu birthday party for Mr. Macdonald on Oct. 4.

"All of the people that love and care about us were around that day," Ms. Macdonald said, as she stared out over the peaceful river valley behind her home.

"We just counted our blessings that we were still alive."

—Cathy von Kintzel

Recovery

TIM KROCHAK

A severed power pole dangles above Windmill Road in Dartmouth on Monday. 'We've never had anything like that before,' said utility president David Mann.

A power struggle of epic proportions

There is a crack
in everything.
That's how the light gets in.
—Leonard Cohen

When they heard a full-scale hurricane was bearing down on the province's biggest city, Nova Scotians in Juan's path expected wind and rain, maybe even some loose shingles or fallen branches.

Most were also counting on the inconvenience of a power outage.

Murray Houghton, whose home in Lawrencetown just metres from the ocean was flooded during hurricane Hortense in 1996, had cleared off his garage floor and was ready to ride out the storm in darkness.

"If you want to live near the ocean, you've got to be prepared to pay the price every now and again when it acts up," he said, as waves pounded the shore, hours before the hurricane hit.

But no one expected the price to be so high.

At the height of the storm, about midnight Sunday, Sept. 28, 300,000 of the 450,000 customers served by Nova Scotia Power Inc. lost their power.

Three-quarters of the province was plunged into a blackout from which some would not emerge for two weeks.

When the scale of the damage became apparent on Sept. 29, Halifax Regional Municipality Mayor Peter Kelly said the city depended on electricity to get back on its feet. "Power, power, power. So much hinges on restoring power service."

Nova Scotia Power was in high gear two days before Juan arrived, entering "storm mode" on Sept. 26. The province's main supplier of electricity stocked up on supplies, arranged a storm management team and had crews on standby around Nova Scotia.

Still, they had no idea how bad it would be.

"We've never had anything like that before," said utility president David Mann. "It's like it was designed to come straight up the harbour, (and) attack the major population and the transmission system in its entirety."

When managers saw how bad the damage was, the company called in crews from New Brunswick and Maine. Up to 1,000 Canadian Forces members took to the streets of Halifax to clear debris so power crews could get to work.

Nova Scotia Power's generating stations escaped serious damage, but every other component of the network was hit hard.

Nancy Tower, general manager of customer service, later described how crews raced to rebuild crumpled transmission towers and bring on main lines, then began the enormous task of restoring power neighbourhood by neighbourhood, block by block.

By the afternoon of the 29th, almost half of those who'd lost power were back online.

But that still left 185,000 in the dark.

For some, the first 24 hours were an adventure. The most pressing need was hot coffee.

Other people foresaw a longer wait for power and stripped store shelves of supplies.

"Generators, pumps and chainsaws are like gold today," said Richard Crosby of Classic Rentals in Truro. "We can't keep up with the demand."

By the last day of September, the blackout wasn't much fun anymore. Schools and most workplaces remained closed, and food was spoiling in fridges and freezers.

Deanna Landry of London Street in Halifax packed it in and headed to Prince Edward Island to stay with her parents.

"Day 1 was OK because we barbecued and had supper on the deck and it was all very exciting, but now the hot water tank is dry and I just can't see the power being back on by tomorrow," she said.

Early on Sept. 30, tragedy struck.

A young mother and two of her children were killed in a fire believed to have been caused by candles. Mary Sack, 22, her son Zachary, 3, and daughter Samia, 2, died in their townhouse, part of a public housing complex. Her husband, Billy Amro, and daughter Anna, 5, were badly injured.

Their wired-in smoke detectors weren't working to warn them of the blaze.

Officials blamed at least four smaller fires on the candles many people relied on for light.

The poor and the elderly suffered most without power. Monthly income-assistance, disability and pension cheques came out just before the storm. Many people had stocked up a month's worth of food only to throw most out days later with no money to replace it.

As the week wore on, power became the only topic of conversation. By mid-week, almost one-quarter of the province was still powerless. Getting it back wasn't just a relief; it was a cause for celebration.

"On our street, families all went to one house, and then when the power came on everybody was screaming — you could hear it up and down the street," said Corinne Abraham of Clearview Drive in Bedford.

Nova Scotia Power workers were hailed as saviours, and crews working 16- and 18-hour shifts said they were sorry they couldn't plow on.

"There's nothing any worse than seeing them looking out their windows as you drive by and you're at the end of your shift," lineman Mike Burtt said.

The people they brought online didn't spare their gratitude.

Continued on next page

Hugs and food for the power boys

TED PRITCHARD

A lineman in a cherry picker works to restore power at the corner of North and King streets in Halifax.

Continued from previous page

"We roll into some streets and there's tables set up with water and food on them if we're hungry," said scoper Scott Cherry. "We put a lady on yesterday, an 89-year-old lady in the north end, she came out and gave me and the guys in the crew all a hug."

It wasn't easy on the families of the men out repairing the wires.

Karen Ferguson went almost two weeks without seeing her husband. John, a lineman for 25 years, was up and gone every day while she was still asleep, and returned long after she went to bed.

"He leaves at five or six in the morning and he gets home around midnight," she said.

Workers on the street were loved, but with thousands lingering in the dark, company officials were not.

At an Oct. 2 news briefing, Nova Scotia Power's Chris Huskilson made a pledge that quickly became a mantra, turning up in company advertisements by the weekend: "Let me assure you that Nova Scotia Power will not rest until every customer is online."

But patience wore out as people heard contradictory stories when they managed to get through to the swamped power outage hotline to ask when their lights might be back on.

"I'm tired of being lied to by Nova Scotia Power," Victoria Dunbrack of Musquodoboit Harbour said on her seventh day without power. "If they'd told us that it would be next Friday that we'd actually get our power back, we could have dealt with that. But they've been telling us, 'Oh, two hours' all week."

Many gave up on the company and called The Herald instead. Jay Jarvis, a university student living in one of six blacked-out houses in an otherwise powered-up south-end neighbourhood, called Oct. 5, fearing he'd been forgotten. "I wonder if they even know."

The worry and anger were compounded by rumours — there was an equipment shortage; the repairs were stop-gaps that would have to be redone; people who had an "in" with the company had been living the high life with hot showers and television for days.

But Nova Scotia Power spokeswoman Margaret Murphy said the job was progressing smoothly, if slowly.

She'd been forced to call the hotline like everyone else and was still without power a week after hurricane Juan.

The remaining isolated pockets of powerless customers would be the most difficult to bring back online, she cautioned.

As anger mounted, Nova Scotia Power officials headed out door to door to speak to people who were still days away from having electricity.

But the end was finally in sight.

Thirteen days after hurricane Juan, Porters Lake and Lake Echo were the last communities to regain the luxury of hot home-cooked meals. Even then, individual houses from Ship Harbour to Cole Harbour were still waiting to be hooked up.

They were dark days, and darker nights, for people everywhere along the hurricane's path. But those days will be remembered vividly.

—John Gillis with Patricia Brooks, Randy Jones, Lois Legge, Bill Power, Bill Spurr and Beverley Ware

Grateful residents of Eastern Passage showed their gratitude to the crews working 18-hour days with a spray-painted sign made out of an old table.

Soldiers clear leaves and branches from Young Avenue in Halifax. More than 1,000 soldiers and sailors were involved in the cleanup.

It left a really, really, really big mess

The weather helped — sunny, warm and calm — as Nova Scotians faced the multimillion-dollar task of cleaning up after Juan.

The yawning roofs of the Cathedral Church of All Saints in Halifax and of Tallahassee Community School in Eastern Passage. Homes all but obliterated by fallen trees. Wharfs wiped out by the dozens in seaside communities. Piles of broken glass; heaps of branches; stacks of shingles. Furniture ruined by wind-driven rain.

The repair bill, said Nova Scotia Premier John Hamm: more than $100 million.

No time was lost getting started on the cleanup, as Forces members and reservists joined provincial and municipal crews in the first hours of Sept. 29. More than 1,000 soldiers and sailors would be involved.

Officials co-ordinating the cleanup found themselves with more hands than plans. Some municipal workers and military reservists were cleaning up parks and cemeteries even as homeowners struggled to move fallen trees off power lines.

Darin Sweet and two of his employees were sawing through the trunk of a tree that had fallen against his six-unit apartment building, tearing power lines and blocking an entrance.

"Obviously, there will be some candle-burning and lamp burning, and I want to make sure if something happens, they can get out and get out fast," he said.

In the next two days, hundreds of sailors and soldiers moved onto the streets of Halifax and Dartmouth to tackle the mess.

At the Dartmouth Sportsplex, the 33 Halifax Service Battalion reservists set up a kitchen to feed displaced residents.

Kyrell Duplexes, 12, who stayed at the Sportsplex shelter, remarked: "I'm not missing home too much." He showed off the sticker that Lt.-Col. Fred Donaldson had used to make him his deputy. "They've been feeding us really great. No complaints!"

About 200 of the 360 reservists even decided to stay on after their group was released Oct. 5.

There were challenges, but also support.

Parishioners of the Cathedral Church of All Saints faced the fact that the church will likely be closed until Christmas. The storm ripped off part of the roof, and rain poured inside.

In Dartmouth, Jennifer Frame sat under a blue tarp that now serves as the roof of the home she bought in March. The single mother, on a disability pension, is getting about $1,100 from her insurance company, leaving her almost nothing for labour and interior repairs. But Ms. Frame contacted Reach Nova Scotia, which helps people with disabilities. There may be someone to work on the roof for whatever she can pay.

Some folks had community cleanup parties — cutting wood and dragging branches to the curbside, "then having a barbecue afterwards," Truro Mayor Bill Mills said.

Colchester County residents also wanted curbside service — but no go. "We're 95 times bigger than Truro and it would cost a fortune, but I do understand people's frustration," Mayor Mike Smith said. "We had 40 trees down in my yard. Five landed on my house and three on my car, so I can totally empathize."

Junior Theriault, a rookie MLA "wiped out" by a storm more than 25 years ago, heard about the plight of hundreds of fishermen and called some former lobster-fishing pals.

"We thought about the fishermen up here, having to go out in another month and how are they going to get their gear," he said in Three Fathom Harbour, after helping Digby lobsterman Richard Gaudet unload donated lobster traps.

"Fishermen are competitive, but this is when being Nova Scotians comes through, people trying to help out as best they can," said Eastern Shore fisherman Dave Theriault, whose wharf repairs and new gear will cost more than $50,000.

It was almost two weeks before the last of 56,000 Halifax-area students kept out of class by Juan got back to school. Justess Crawley, 7, in Grade 2 at Bicentennial School in Dartmouth, had one — perhaps surprising — complaint: "I wish we got homework now."

Most of the 137 schools in the Halifax region had some damage. Students at Tallahassee Community School in Eastern Passage were to split-shift with nearby Seaside Elementary for about two months, awaiting roof repairs.

During the hiatus, unfortunately, some young people went awry, even throwing rocks at cleanup crews. In one 24-hour period, Halifax police responded to 38 complaints, while RCMP had dozens of complaints in suburban areas about kids smashing windows, harassing outside workers and setting brush fires.

And finally, politicians began to grapple with the cost of what will be a months-long, even years-long cleanup task.

Prime Minister Jean Chretien didn't come to visit Nova Scotia — which angered many — so Premier John Hamm went to see him in Ottawa on Oct. 9 to discuss relief funding.

"You know, we sent troops there and some ministers," Mr. Chretien said.

Mr. Hamm backed up the prime minister, pointing out that Defence Minister John McCallum, who oversees the disaster relief program, and Fisheries Minister Robert Thibault, Nova Scotia's cabinet representative, were in Halifax just a few days after Juan.

—John Gillis, Barry Dorey, David Jackson, Rick Conrad, Mary Ellen MacIntyre, Randy Jones, Dan Arsenault, Davene Jeffrey, Beverley Ware and Brian Underhill

Waiting for the next crop of trees

Catastrophes leave special marks on individuals and communities. Seventy or eighty years from now, there will still be people who vividly remember when they were children and the world suddenly went upside down.

They might have trembled in their beds for a few wild hours the night of Sept. 28, 2003, heard huge crashes, felt the rising concern and perhaps the incipient panic of the adults around them. When they rose in the morning, it might have seemed the whole world had been uprooted and beaten by a rampaging giant.

Some will have fond memories of that day and the days that followed — a time when they played amid the wreckage, when neighbours gathered for barbecues because the power was out, when people helped one another, when the scars on the physical world were compensated for by the falling of invisible human barriers.

They will be reminded of the event by the presence of trees in some places that haven't been removed but remain there rotting for decades.

Most Nova Scotians of a certain age have a special storm they remember as the children of today will remember Juan. Mine was Edna, in 1954, when I was 11 years old; it went through western Nova Scotia and up the Bay of Fundy.

Such events become sort of historical markers.

Edna came up in conversation only a few months ago. I was contemplating a strip of wood in Yarmouth County that had recently been cut. I remembered it as having been flattened by Edna. "You mean to tell me we've had a crop of trees here already since Edna?" I asked a friend. "How time flies."

If individuals are marked, communities are as well. Ways of thinking change. The social psychology is rattled by such sudden and unforeseen fury, and questions become prominent that were only marginal before. What are the chances of it happening again in the not-too-distant future? How do we better prepare if it does?

There is, of course, no answer to the if and when. For one thing, the part of the Atlantic coast that can get hit runs from Central America to Newfoundland, and many hurricanes miss it altogether (a few degrees to the left or the right, and Juan would have spared Halifax). Unless you live along the strip from Florida to Virginia and parts of the Gulf of Mexico, your chances of getting hit, until recently, have been very slight.

But now the odds may be higher. Since warm ocean water is a factor in the number and intensity of hurricanes, global warming is something to think about.

Hurricanes usually weaken as they hit the cold water of the North Atlantic. But with the water much warmer than normal, that expectation may no longer be valid. Indeed, in merely asking about global warming, Nova Scotia joins jurisdictions from Florida to Virginia, which have been taking direct hits with increasing frequency and intensity over the past couple of decades.

The questions, there as here, have to do with infrastructure: How and where do you build in order to withstand the next shot? The hazards of high winds will be — or at least ought to be — on the minds of planners of all sorts from now on.

With regard to the vulnerable electrical grid, the possibility of burying more power lines arises, as does the installation of other wind-resistant security measures. According to an agriculture official, silos, some of which toppled, are unlikely to be built vertically anymore. "Bagged silage" fermented in low buildings was already the new way, but Juan added a security incentive to that method.

Along the coast, where the hazards of the wind are better known, the ferocity of Juan still caught people unprepared and destroyed fishing gear, boats, wharfs, buildings — whole fishing villages torn to pieces. "The next blow" will be on the minds of those rebuilding, including government engineers, for a long time to come.

Great chunks of a vast swath of forest were also flattened, starting at Point Pleasant Park at the tip of the Halifax peninsula and running through central Nova Scotia to the Northumberland shore. Although little can be done about protecting mature trees in the wild from wind, the future of the urban forest in tree-proud Halifax provides some interesting considerations.

It was trees — those huge, ancient and top-heavy sylvan beings — that caused most of the damage and even killed two people. For Haligonians — for Nova Scotians — to see their stately trees as dangerous is a wrenching twist, and one that could sustain debate for some time.

If the city had done more pruning, or if work crews were trained not to cut roots when they installed sidewalks, trees wouldn't have been so vulnerable, say critics. But pruning costs money, as does burying power lines and building stronger roofs.

At any rate, it's likely that whenever a power company crew shows up to cut some trees that are a threat to power lines, the neighbourhood protests won't be half as vociferous as they used to be. And with so many big ones down, Nova Scotians will have to learn to love the young and growing ones.

It even touches on that deepest of Canadian issues: Are hurricanes a federal or provincial matter? In this case, the issue is who will pay.

We can only hope that argument won't last as long as it takes to grow the next crop of trees — or drag on until the next hurricane hits.

—**Ralph Surette**

'He who plants a tree, plants a hope.'
— Lucy Larcom

Pat MacLean and her granddaughter Taylor plant a white spruce sapling in the backyard of Mrs. MacLean's Spryfield home to replace a maple knocked down by hurricane Juan.

CHRISTIAN LAFORCE

This book is dedicated
to the memory of
Stephen Munro,
John Rossiter,
Mary Sack,
Zachary Sack-Amro
and Samia Sack-Amro